CW01111710

Original title:
You Deserve To Be Happy

Copyright © 2024 Book Fairy Publishing
All rights reserved.

Editor: Theodor Taimla
Author: Hanna Helimets
ISBN HARDBACK: 978-9916-756-70-6
ISBN PAPERBACK: 978-9916-756-71-3

Delightful Revelations

In twilight's gentle whisper, dreams unfold,
Secrets of the night in silver tone,
Leading hearts where stories oft retold,
Echo softly in the moonlit zone.

Stars above, they twinkle, secrets share,
Guiding us to paths yet to be known,
Moments cherished in the cool night air,
Where time's illusions gently are overthrown.

By the firelight, shadows softly sway,
Tales of yore in embers bravely glow,
Eyes meet eyes, and souls break free away,
In these moments, love's own seeds we sow.

Illumination from Within

In silence, depths of self unveil,
Wisdom blooms where shadows once hid,
Subtle light in heart's deep well,
Guides the soul through paths amid.

Quiet whispers of the inner voice,
Echo in the stillness of the mind,
Revealing truths in their poised choice,
From the night, enlightenment we find.

A sacred glow ignites the heart,
Lighting dreams that once were blurred,
With every beat, a fresh new start,
And inner peace in silence heard.

Everyday Miracles

Morning dew on blades of grass,
Tiny gems that greet the day,
Miracles in moments pass,
Simple wonders in our way.

Birds in chorus greet the dawn,
Symphonies of nature play,
Every note a fleeting song,
Elegance in their array.

Kindness in a stranger's smile,
Shared with warmth around we see,
Miracles in every mile,
Every step, a mystery.

Eternal Merriment

Laughter echoes through the hall,
Joyous hearts in mirth unite,
Songs of cheer in voices call,
Radiance in the warmest light.

Dance of life in blissful spin,
Moments filled with boundless glee,
Eternal smiles that start within,
Bound by love's own decree.

Festive spirits soar so high,
Hearts embrace the rhythm bright,
In gleeful waves, our worries fly,
Hence, souls uplifted in delight.

Glimmers of Pure Bliss

In a world where stars align,
Hearts converge, moments twine.
Glimmers of pure bliss arise,
Love within, no disguise.

Meadows green, skies so blue,
Whispers soft, feelings true.
Laughter echoes in the night,
Moonlit paths, soft and bright.

Timeless dances, gentle sway,
Dreams unfold, fears allay.
In pure joy's tender embrace,
Find our place, seek no trace.

Eternal Radiance

Radiant beams warm the soul,
Eternal light, make us whole.
Through the shadows, brilliance gleams,
Sews our hearts with golden seams.

Sacred flames in twilight's haze,
Burning brightly, love's true blaze.
Guidance found in steady glow,
Ebbing tides, we gently flow.

In the expanse of the night,
Stars align, shine so bright.
Eternal radiance prevails,
In our hearts, love unveils.

Cherished Moments

In the quiet of the morn,
Love's first light, there reborn.
Cherished moments, fleeting, sweet,
Every heartbeat, love replete.

Whispers soft and hands entwined,
In those eyes, peace we find.
Time stands still, joy unbound,
Precious smiles, love profound.

Captured glimpses, hearts align,
In your presence, our light shines.
In life's tapestry, we weave,
Cherished moments, never leave.

Echoes of Bliss

Through the valley, over hills,
Echoes of bliss, the heart fills.
Soft serenades, whispers light,
Dance of love, pure and bright.

In the stillness, love remains,
Gentle touch, soothing strains.
Memories etched, moments kissed,
Life's sweet echoes, hearts won't miss.

In each dawn, we start anew,
In love's radiance, skies so blue.
Echoes of bliss, fill our days,
In their warmth, forever stay.

Pure Rapture

In the stillness of night, whispers of stars,
Gently caress dreams, near or far.
A cascade of light, through heaven's gate,
Guides the soul to a tranquil state.

Waves of emotion, tenderly sweep,
Through valleys of wonder, and oceans deep.
Ethereal chords, a celestial choir,
Ignites the heart with boundless fire.

In the embrace of moon's tender glow,
Secrets of the cosmos softly grow.
Enigmatic tides in perfect capture,
Reveal the dance of pure rapture.

Melody of Merriment

Sunlight gilds the morning dew,
Awakening the skies to hues anew.
Birds exclaim in joyous rounds,
Delighting in nature's harmonious sounds.

Laughter echoes through the air,
Twinkling eyes a spark declare.
Dancing leaves on a gentle breeze,
Whisper secrets through the trees.

As day unfurls in golden streams,
Life sways in a rhythm of dreams.
Beneath the canopy of heaven's tent,
Sings the melody of merriment.

Spring of Delight

A blushing dawn in soft pastel,
Bathes the earth in a tender spell.
Blossoms burst with fragrant might,
Heralding the spring of delight.

Rivers dance in silver light,
Flowing freely day and night.
Whispers of the blooming seed,
Promise of a world to heed.

Nature's palette, rich and wide,
Cloaks the earth in verdant pride.
Every leaf and petal bright,
Sings the song of pure delight.

Harmony Unleashed

Soft symphony of rustling leaves,
Blends with the whispering breeze.
In the forest's heart, a tranquil peace,
Unfurls in the harmony unleashed.

Mountains echo, valleys reply,
To the symphonic sky on high.
Nature's chords in unison play,
The timeless song of a brand new day.

In the heartbeats of ancient trees,
Reside the notes of life's reprise.
Each living soul eternally reached,
Through life's song, harmony unleashed.

Peaceful Waters

Beneath the tranquil sky,
Where gentle whispers flow,
Waters weave a lullaby,
Soft as morning's glow.

Ripples kiss the shore,
With tender, soothing grace,
Endless stories they implore,
In nature's calm embrace.

Sunlight dances bright,
Across the surface clear,
In a symphony of light,
Filling hearts with cheer.

Beneath the shaded trees,
Breaths grow deep and slow,
In the ever gentle breeze,
Peaceful waters know.

Echoes of the day,
Fade into the night,
Waters gently play,
In the moon's soft light.

Songs of Exultation

Voices pure and bright,
Rise with morning's sun,
Melodies take flight,
A new day has begun.

Harmonies that soar,
To the heavens high,
In a joyous roar,
They touch the sky.

Hearts are lifted up,
In a grand refrain,
Overflowing cup,
Of love's sweet gain.

Every note is free,
Echoes through the land,
In unity, they plea,
Hand in tender hand.

Songs of exultation,
Fill the air with cheer,
In this celebration,
Every soul draws near.

The Enchanted Smile

In the moon's soft glow,
A secret lies concealed,
A smile begins to show,
Magic is revealed.

Eyes that gently gleam,
With a silent grace,
Like a tender dream,
Wearing joy's embrace.

Innocence and light,
In every fleeting glance,
Enchanting the night,
With love's sweet chance.

Lips that whisper hope,
In every wordless sigh,
Teaching hearts to cope,
With wings that fly.

In an enchanted smile,
Worlds are born anew,
A mystery all the while,
Pure and ever true.

Golden Dreams

In the starlit night,
Dreams begin to weave,
Threads of golden light,
In minds that believe.

Whispers of delight,
Guide each dreamer's way,
Through the velvet night,
Till the break of day.

Visions pure and bright,
Fill the resting heart,
In this gentle flight,
Worlds of wonder start.

Hope and joy entwine,
In a dreamer's gaze,
Tasting the divine,
In the golden rays.

Golden dreams unfold,
With a tender gleam,
In their magic hold,
Life is but a dream.

Brilliance in Being

In the quiet dawn's embrace,
A spark ignites the soul.
Through life's uncharted space,
We journey toward the whole.

Each step, a dance in time,
A rhythm purely ours.
The climb, though steep and prime,
Reveals unmeasured powers.

In moments, vast and tender,
The heart learns how to see,
Beauty's bright, untamed splendor,
Crafted ingeniously.

Embrace the silent knowing,
As stars weave tales above,
The brilliance ever-growing,
In the canvas of our love.

Be present in this being,
Where infinite lights reside,
In the act of simply seeing,
Our dreams and truths collide.

The Shining Path

Upon a trail of golden light,
We tread with hearts unbound.
Through shadows of the endless night,
A guiding star is found.

Whispers of the ancient trees,
Confide in us their lore.
With every step, the spirit frees,
And dares to seek for more.

Mirrors in the moonlit stream,
Reflect our inner sight.
Harbingers of vivid dreams,
Illuminate the night.

As dawn unfolds with tender hues,
Untold horizons greet.
The path before us gently woos,
Our never-fearing feet.

Together on this shining path,
We find our true embrace.
In joy and in the aftermath,
Our spirits interlace.

A Beacon of Bliss

In realms where dreams alight,
A beacon calls our soul.
Eclipsing fears of night,
It guides to make us whole.

In fields of fragrant daisies,
Where laughter meets the breeze,
We wander through life's mazes,
With hearts that feel at ease.

The sky a canvas painted,
With hues both bright and bold.
In bliss, we're unabated,
Our stories, new and old.

In every fleeting moment,
A spark of joy we find.
Through change and firm atonement,
Our spirits are aligned.

This beacon of pure bliss,
An everlasting friend.
In every smile and kiss,
Its light shall never end.

Inner Sunshine

Beneath the clouds of weary day,
A warmth begins to rise.
Through trials, come what may,
The light within us flies.

In stillness, it awakens,
This sun beneath our skin.
No storm can make it shaken,
Its strength starts from within.

A glow in every action,
A smile that gently beams.
In moments of reflection,
It fuels our brightest dreams.

When shadows cast their longing,
And paths seem cold and bare,
This sunshine keeps us strong,
In every breath and prayer.

So, kindle this inner light,
Let love's pure rays unfold.
Through darkest days or night,
Our sunshine stands bold.

Light Beyond Shadows

In the cavern of dark, where silence keeps,
A whisper of hope, quietly creeps.
Upon each shadow, a gentle light,
Seeping through the cracks of night.

Beneath the veil, where demons tread,
Softly shines what they most dread.
Courage born in the heart so fine,
Turning gloom to thoughts divine.

Even the night must make its way,
For dawn will break at the end of day.
Shadow fades where the light does flow,
From the deepest dark to the ember glow.

Inner Sunlight

Within the core, light deeply lies,
Shining past the world's disguise.
In every soul, a sun doth seed,
Spreading warmth through every deed.

Shadows pale, where this light shines,
Igniting hearts with fiery lines.
No storm can quell this inner gleam,
Nor quiet the resilient dream.

Through the trials, fierce and long,
The sunlight sings a steadfast song.
Oft unseen, yet ever bright,
Guiding through the darkest night.

Hearts in Harmony

A rhythm shared within the heart,
Beats aligned though miles apart.
Unified through love's sweet chord,
Harmony is its own reward.

Echoes merge through time and space,
Creating bonds no force can chase.
Laughter, tears, both resonate,
Crafting tunes both mild and great.

In every note, connection grows,
In harmonic waves it flows.
Love composes its own lore,
Bringing souls to dance once more.

Jubilee of Joy

A symphony of laughter fills the air,
In every heart, joy blooms with care.
Moments bright, pure delight,
Turning darkness into light.

Happiness, like rivers, stream,
Creating life from every dream.
Diadems of sunshine gleam,
Binding us in joy's bright seam.

Celebrate with open hearts,
In joy, we're never far apart.
Spirits high, like stars above,
A jubilee of boundless love.

The Dawn of Cheerfulness

The sun peeks over hills afar,
A golden hue, a morning star,
Whispers of joy in the morning breeze,
Lifting spirits with gentle ease.

Birds sing sweet melodies anew,
Flowers awaken with morning dew,
Hearts once heavy, now so light,
Embrace the dawn, a hopeful sight.

Cherished moments start to glow,
Casting shadows long and low,
In every gaze, a spark so clear,
The dawn of cheer is finally here.

Smiles blossom like the morning rose,
In worry's place, pure laughter grows,
A brand new day, a vibrant sphere,
Welcomes us with cheer sincere.

With each sunrise, the spirit soars,
Unlocking life's boundless doors,
In the dawn, a promise bright,
Cheerfulness, our guiding light.

Cascades of Laughter

Laughter flows like a crystal stream,
In twilight hours or morning's beam,
Echoes of joy fill the air,
Dispelling gloom, dispelling care.

Glimmers of laughter, pure and bright,
Dance like stars in the endless night,
Moments shared, hearts align,
Under skies both dark and kind.

Ripples of mirth spread far and wide,
As worries wane, tears subside,
A river of joy, unceasing, grand,
Flows through every heart, every land.

In the cadence of a friend's delight,
The world feels lighter, spirits take flight,
Echoes merge, a symphony,
Cascades of laughter, wild and free.

Bridges built on beams of glee,
Unite us all, hold us in spree,
The world transforms with every sound,
Of laughter's echo, so profound.

Harmony in Every Breath

With every breath, a symphony,
Lives entwined in harmony,
Nature whispers, soft and clear,
A gentle song for all to hear.

Leaves that rustle in the breeze,
A melody that sets minds at ease,
Waters ripple, skies extend,
In every breath, the earth's amend.

Heartbeats echo, time aligns,
Weaving through the grand designs,
In silence or in joyous sound,
Harmony in breaths is found.

Moments fleeting, sighs released,
Bringing home a gentle peace,
A world in balance, truth be told,
In every breath, it's grace we hold.

Life's symphony, both soft and strong,
Plays the tune where we belong,
Inhale deeply, feel the blend,
Harmony in every breath, my friend.

Radiance Within

Inside each heart, a light so bright,
Even amidst the deepest night,
A beacon of hope, a star unspun,
Radiance within, outshines the sun.

Moments of doubt may cloud the sky,
Yet the inner light will never die,
It thrives in joy, endures in pain,
An eternal flame, through loss and gain.

In smiles shared and kindness shown,
The inner glow is truly known,
A touch of grace, a spark divine,
In every soul, a light does shine.

Through shadows dark and paths unseen,
Our inner light remains serene,
Guiding us through trials and test,
With radiance, we manifest.

Embrace the glow, let shadows flee,
The light within sets spirits free,
In every heart, this truth we find,
Radiance within, so intertwined.

Eternity of Light

In skies where stardust gleams,
A realm of endless beams,
Eternal light unfolds,
In stories, yet untold.

A dawn that never dies,
Where night melts into skies,
A dance of twilight's grace,
In time's eternal chase.

Each beam a whisper's plea,
A song of what could be,
In cosmic tapestries,
Our souls find destinies.

Beyond the edge of fear,
A faith that's ever near,
In light, our shadows fade,
In hope, new dawns are made.

Through realms of sacred dreams,
Where light forever streams,
We journey, hearts alight,
In search of endless light.

Waves of Tranquility

On shores of silent grace,
Where waves in soft embrace,
Whisper their lullabies,
Beneath the azure skies.

By tranquil seas we sit,
In moments deeply lit,
With echoes of the past,
In memories that last.

The ocean's tender sweep,
A cradle as we sleep,
In rhythms of the deep,
Our souls, the calm to keep.

The tides that come and go,
In gentle ebb and flow,
A symphony so bright,
In serenade of night.

Within the sea's vast heart,
Our spirits find their part,
In waves of pure serene,
Where peace is evergreen.

The Gleeful Quest

In lands where dreams do lie,
Beneath an open sky,
A trail of joy we seek,
In moments bold and meek.

Through woods of whispering trees,
In laughter carried by breeze,
We wander without rest,
In search of gleeful quest.

With hearts of boundless cheer,
No sorrow do we fear,
As sunlight guides our way,
To find a brighter day.

Each step a story's page,
With life our vibrant stage,
In joy, we move along,
Our hearts, the endless song.

The journey endless seems,
Fueled by our vivid dreams,
In quest of gleeful light,
We find our souls take flight.

Rays of Warmth

In morn's first gentle glance,
Where sunlight starts to dance,
Rays of warmth unfold,
In hues of liquid gold.

Among the fields we rove,
Beneath the skies above,
In touch of sunlight's grace,
We find a warm embrace.

Through every leaf and bloom,
In nature's quiet room,
The golden streams cascade,
In shades no light can fade.

In hearts where hope does gleam,
As sunlight's softest beam,
Rays of warmth ignite,
The coldest soul to light.

With every dawn we rise,
Beneath these endless skies,
In rays of warmth, we find,
A love that binds mankind.

Joy Is Your Birthright

In the hush of morning light,
Where dreams and hope ignite,
Feel the warmth within your chest,
Joy is yours, and you are blessed.

Beyond the clouds, the sun does gleam,
In every heart's secret dream,
Hold its light, embrace its grace,
Joy enshrines your sacred space.

In laughter's echo, joy is found,
In kindness given all around,
Cherish these, for they are true,
Joy belongs inside of you.

When shadows fall and doubts arise,
Lift your gaze to azure skies,
Carry joy in heart and mind,
It's your birthright, pure, divine.

Peace and love, they intertwine,
In your spirit, softly shine,
Through the dark and through the bright,
Know that joy is your birthright.

A Garden of Smiles

In a garden full of blooms,
Where sunlight gently looms,
Smiles are petals on the breeze,
Warmed by whispers in the trees.

Laughter like a babbling brook,
In every cranny, every nook,
Spreads a joy so pure and wild,
A garden that has always smiled.

Each blossom tells a story bright,
Of hope and love, a pure delight,
Colors dance within your eyes,
In this garden, no disguise.

Touch the petals, feel the cheer,
Banish all your lurking fears,
Every flower shares its light,
Smiles bloom day and night.

In this place where dreams reside,
Walk with joy, let hearts collide,
In a garden of pure smiles,
Find your peace for countless miles.

Sunlight in Your Soul

Amidst the dawn, a glow appears,
Washing away the night's last fears,
Gently, warmly, it unfolds,
Feel the sunlight in your soul.

In every step, in every glance,
There lies a hidden, shining dance,
Carry forth this radiant goal,
Keep the sunlight in your soul.

When storms arise and dark clouds throng,
Hold steadfast, keep your inner song,
Light's eternal, pure and whole,
Burn the sunlight in your soul.

Through valleys deep and mountains high,
Let your spirit touch the sky,
Guide your heart where dreams extol,
For there's sunlight in your soul.

With every sunset, every ray,
Embrace the gift of each new day,
In your being, make it whole,
Nurture sunlight in your soul.

Whispers of Bliss

In the quietude of night,
When stars adorn the endless height,
Listen close, and you shall see,
Blissful whispers, wild and free.

Through the rustle of the leaves,
In the sighs the wind believes,
Hear the murmurs, sweet and low,
Whispers of bliss start to grow.

In a smile, a touch so light,
In a dream that takes to flight,
Feel the magic, feel the kiss,
Softly comes the blissful whisper.

In the moments still and calm,
Find the soothing, healing balm,
Happiness, it plants its kiss,
In the tender, whispered bliss.

Through the silence, through the day,
Let the whispers show the way,
In your heart, eternal bliss,
Hold these whispers, feel their kiss.

Uplifted Spirit

In the dawn, my soul takes flight,
Far beyond the reach of night.
With hope as wings, I soar so high,
Above the world, I meet the sky.

Mountains whisper secrets deep,
Valleys in quiet slumber sleep.
Embrace the wind, embrace the air,
Feel the love that's everywhere.

Eyes alight with dreams so vast,
Heart beats strong, the shadows past.
Rise above the fears and strife,
To find the light that frees your life.

Bow to Happiness

In fields of gold, where daisies bloom,
I find a place without a gloom.
Underneath the azure sky,
Happiness sings a lullaby.

Echoes of laughter fill the air,
Joyful hearts without a care.
Bow to the sun, so warm and bright,
In its glow, we find our light.

In every smile, in every glance,
We share a timeless, joyous dance.
Happiness, a gentle breeze,
Bringing comfort, bringing ease.

Blossoming Radiance

Petals unfurl with morning dew,
The beauty of life comes into view.
Each blossom tells a tale of grace,
A radiant smile on nature's face.

Sunbeams kiss the flowers' cheeks,
In this paradise, love speaks.
Soft whispers of a gentle breeze,
Wrap us in tender, soothing ease.

Nature's colors, vivid and bright,
Fill our hearts with sheer delight.
In this garden of life's design,
We find a peace, pure and divine.

Freedom in Joy

The chains that bind, I cast aside,
In joy's embrace, I now reside.
With every breath, my spirit sings,
Soaring high on freedom's wings.

Fields of green beneath my feet,
Where hearts in joy may always meet.
Running wild, free as the air,
Living life without a care.

Laughter echoes through the trees,
Life's vibrant, endless melodies.
In joy, we find the keys to be,
Our truest selves, in harmony.

Embrace the Light

In the morning's gentle glow,
Hues of gold begin to show,
Chasing shadows of the night,
Inviting hearts to embrace the light.

Whispers of the dawn arise,
Hope reflected in our eyes,
With every beam that meets our gaze,
We find new strength in sunlit days.

The world awakens from its sleep,
Promises and dreams to keep,
A canvas painted fresh and bright,
Where souls are free to take flight.

In the warmth of day's embrace,
We uncover joy and grace,
Every moment shines anew,
Guiding us to paths so true.

Shimmering Horizons

On the horizon, dreams take flight,
Silver streaks through darkest night,
A world of wonder lies ahead,
As lights begin to softly spread.

Beyond the reach of sight and sound,
Endless landscapes to be found,
Each shimmering with a distant gleam,
A treasure map for every dream.

The twilight whispers lullabies,
As stars ignite the velvet skies,
Guiding hearts to realms unknown,
Where seeds of hope and magic sown.

In every glow, a story told,
Of adventures brave and hearts so bold,
Horizons shimmer, calling near,
Inviting us to lose all fear.

Happiness Calls

In the laughter of a child,
In moments gentle and so mild,
Happiness calls from deep within,
A precious gift where joys begin.

Through the echoes of a song,
In places where we all belong,
It dances lightly through the air,
A whisper saying, "Do not despair."

With every smile and tender glance,
It offers yet another chance,
To find delight in simple things,
And soar on high with unseen wings.

When shadows seem to cloud our sight,
And days are void of pure delight,
Remember well that happiness calls,
Ever-present within life's halls.

Brilliant Horizons

As the dawn begins to break,
Dreamers rise and pathways take,
To horizons brilliant and wide,
Where new adventures lie inside.

Every sunrise paints the sky,
With colors bold and spirits high,
A symphony of light and grace,
That leads us to a wondrous place.

The journey calls with whispered pleas,
Through forests dense and ancient seas,
Each step a promise of the new,
In lands where hopes and wishes true.

The road may bend and twist around,
Yet in the heart, a song profound,
Of brilliant horizons yet to see,
A future bright for you and me.

Chasing Sunrises

In the quiet dawn's first light
We chase the day from darkest night
With hopes that bask in hues of gold
New stories, yet to be told

Mountains dark, we leave behind
Sunrise calling, hearts aligned
Each step forward, into the glow
Promises of day unfold, we know

Blanket clouds, orange and blue
We chase the moments, fresh and new
Waking world, breath that frees
Chasing sunrises, dreams in breeze

Journey's start, horizon calls
Morning whispers, cradles, falls
Colors bloom, a canvas wide
In this dawn, our spirits glide

Together we seek, the morning true
With every sunrise, life renew
In the chase, we find our place
Sun's embrace, an endless grace

Embrace the Gleam

In the world of shadows, bright
Gleaming stars, our guiding light
To chase the dark with every beam
In hopeful hearts, we find a gleam

Through trials and winds that blow
A steadfast heart, resolves to grow
Glimmers of a brighter dream
In every soul, embrace the gleam

With courage, cast the fears aside
To the light, together we ride
In the ebb of doubt and scream
Love will rise, and so will gleam

The night may fall, shadows spread
Yet gleaming hearts will forge ahead
Hope's eternal, bold as dream
In life's embrace, we'll find the gleam

Beyond the clouds, the stars unseen
A world awaits, serene and keen
In truth and trust, we are the stream
Gleaming bright, we embrace the gleam

Hearts Afloat

On the waves, our hearts set sail
Through the journey, light and frail
With every crest, our spirits swell
Where love's tide and hopes dwell

The sea of dreams, vast and wide
We drift along, side by side
In moonlit nights, stars denote
Guiding us, with hearts afloat

Every whisper, ocean's song
Carries us, no-right, nor wrong
Beneath the sky, dreams both wrote
Together we've, our hearts afloat

Gentle waves, caress the sand
Love like tides, gentle, unplanned
In twilight hues, tales we quote
Eternal bond, two hearts afloat

Journeys end, or just begun
Hearts afloat, beneath sun
Together sail, love's golden boat
Endless sea, our hearts afloat

Inner Radiance

In the mirror of the soul, a glow
Radiance that sets hearts aglow
Beyond the facade, light we trace
Illuminates, the darkest place

Through life's prism, colors blend
Inner light will always send
A beacon bright, pure and true
Guiding us in all we do

Silent whispers, often heard
In the heart, the brightened word
Shining through, each circumstance
Awakens our inner radiance

Through the storm, in shadows deep
Light within, our spirits keep
Faith that rises, dances, prance
Within us, our inner radiance

Let it shine, unshackled, bold
Radiance pure, as story told
In every heart, the chance
To illuminate, with inner radiance

A Soul Liberated

Chains fall away, the dawn breaks clear,
Echoes of past no longer near.
Soft winds whisper dreams once veiled,
Now the spirit soars, untrammeled, hailed.

A horizon gilded by freedom's light,
The weightless steps, so pure, so bright.
In the stillness, courage found,
A soul's true song, unfettered sound.

Gently flows the river's grace,
Each ripple a kiss, a soft embrace.
Emergence from a shadowed place,
Life's new canvas, an open space.

Sunlight dances on the edge,
A future scribed on nature's ledge.
Breath so deep, the air so clear,
To be oneself, without a fear.

Echoes now a distant hum,
With boundless skies, a new day's drum.
The journey etched in stars above,
Liberation, courage, love.

Boundless Euphoria

Fields alight with flowered dreams,
Sunlight in a golden stream.
Euphoria in every stride,
Boundless joy, a gentle guide.

Heartbeats sync with nature's theme,
A tapestry in hues that gleam.
Laughter echoes, wild and free,
In this embrace, eternity.

Stars ignite the twilight's gaze,
In euphoria's tender blaze.
Soft whispers in the evening mist,
Moments like these, forever kissed.

Waves of bliss on gentle shores,
Infinite as love explores.
Boundless as the sky above,
Wrapped in euphoria's tender glove.

Dancing in the moonlit air,
Euphoria, beyond compare.
Heart and soul in perfect flight,
Boundless, endless, pure delight.

Sweet Liberation

Unseen chains that held me tight,
Now dissolve in morning light.
Sweet liberation, fresh as dew,
A world reborn in colors new.

Every step, a tale untold,
Freed from yesterdays of old.
A melody of winds so sweet,
Guiding gently, whispering fleet.

Butterflies in joyful flight,
Mirror my soul's gentle might.
Open skies, horizons vast,
In this freedom, home at last.

Each breath, a song of liberation,
Every moment, a celebration.
Hearts entwined with freedom's grace,
In this journey, find one's place.

Softly sings the morning breeze,
In sweet liberation's ease.
A symphony, the earth and I,
Boundless spirit, soaring high.

Illuminated Heart

In the silence, peace unfolds,
A heart illuminated, bold.
Light's embrace, a gentle start,
Awakens now, an open heart.

Whispers of the moonlit night,
Guide the soul to quiet light.
Inward gaze, a truth so deep,
Stars within, their vigil keep.

Each heartbeat, a sacred note,
In the silence, dreams afloat.
Light within the shadows found,
A heart's true path, profound, unbound.

Embers of the past dissolve,
In love's light, all fears absolve.
An illuminated heart so bright,
Casts away the cloak of night.

Find within, the endless spark,
Guided through the darkest arc.
With an illuminated heart,
Every step, a work of art.

Celebrating Existence

From dawn to dusk, we weave our thread,
In moments lived and dreams ahead.
The sunlit paths, the nights we claim,
Existence dances, a vibrant flame.

Whispers of the stars above,
Echo tales of endless love.
In the bonds of life, we find,
Threads of joy ever entwined.

With hearts aglow in life's embrace,
We cherish every fleeting trace.
Time may pass, yet we remain,
In the heartbeat of the rain.

Celebrating every breath we take,
In the ripples of the shining lake.
For every dawn and every night,
We bask in life's pure, radiant light.

In laughter's echo, tears unplanned,
We hold the world within our hand.
Celebrating all we are,
A journey, near and far.

Elysian Vibes

Beneath the canopy of sky,
Where dreams ascend and spirits fly.
In whispers soft, the world bestows,
The peace that only silence knows.

Fields of gold, a gentle breeze,
Time suspended, moving ease.
Inhale the warmth, exhale the cares,
Elysian vibes in moments rare.

Mountains rise and rivers flow,
Hearts attuned to nature's glow.
Harmony in every glance,
Life unfolds a timeless dance.

In twilight's calm, the world aligns,
Softest hues and sacred signs.
Life in balance, love enshrined,
Elysian vibes in stars confined.

Journey through the realms unknown,
Where beauty breathes and hearts are shown.
In the essence of the night,
Elysian vibes, our souls unite.

The Joy Awakens

In the morning's gentle rise,
Joy awakens, fills the skies.
Sunlight dances, shadows fade,
A new day's promise in brigade.

In the laughter of the dew,
Sparkling worlds come into view.
Blossoms greet with open arms,
Nature's blissful, subtle charms.

Through the chorus of the birds,
Joy transcends in silent words.
Hearts that beat in rhythmic grace,
Joy awakens, finds its place.

Moments gleam with bright delight,
Chasing sorrows out of sight.
With every smile, a story weaves,
A tapestry of joy received.

Under skies so vast and blue,
Life's sweet joy in all we do.
Awake to every precious day,
In joy's embrace, we find our way.

Dawn of Inner Peace

As twilight fades and night departs,
A gentle calm within us starts.
Whispers of the coming light,
A dawn of peace, serene, and bright.

In the stillness of the morn,
Newfound hopes and dreams are born.
Echoes of the night's release,
Usher in a boundless peace.

The world awakes with tender grace,
In the silence, find your place.
In every hue and soft embrace,
The dawn of peace within you trace.

Through gentle mists and waking sighs,
A tranquil spirit softly flies.
In every breath and heart's release,
Discover endless inner peace.

As each new day begins anew,
Hold the peace that comes to you.
In the quiet, find reprieve,
A dawn of peace we shall achieve.

The Luminous Journey

In twilight's tender, guiding hand,
We tread upon the silver sand,
With whispered winds, we understand,
A world of dreams at our command.

Through forests deep, where shadows lie,
We trace the stars upon the sky,
With every step, a gentle sigh,
The night unfolds, our spirits high.

The moonlit path, a gleaming thread,
With mysteries we softly tread,
Each heartbeat like a word unsaid,
In silence, every soul is fed.

Within the realms of pure delight,
We venture forth into the night,
With hearts aglow, our spirits bright,
Embracing all within our sight.

The dawn will rise, and we shall see,
The echoes of our journey free,
A tapestry of memory,
In the light of our destiny.

A Symphony of Smiles

The morning breaks with golden hues,
A melody in every view,
Where joy alights, the world renews,
In every smile, the music's true.

Beneath the sky so vast and clear,
Each laugh a note that we hold dear,
Together, rendering here,
A symphony for all to hear.

In harmony, our voices blend,
The bonds of friendship never end,
With laughter's light, our hearts ascend,
And tender moments we defend.

The day unfolds, a joyous tune,
With sunlit skies from June to June,
In every beam, a sweet commune,
Of grins that lift the afternoon.

As twilight falls with gentle grace,
We find our place, a warm embrace,
Upon each face, no dark can trace,
A symphony, a smile's embrace.

Elation in the Air

Within the dawn's first breath so fair,
Awakens joy beyond compare,
With every step, a love affair,
Elation dances in the air.

Through meadows wide, where flowers bloom,
Their petals burst, dispelling gloom,
In nature's song, a sweet perfume,
Our hearts take flight, no more to resume.

With each embrace, the world is bright,
A tapestry of pure delight,
Our souls entwined, a feathered kite,
In skies so clear, a boundless sight.

The laughter shared, a tender sound,
Within our spirits, we have found,
A joy profound, no ties to ground,
A boundless love that knows no bound.

As evening hues the sky with gold,
In each embrace, a warmth untold,
Together, hands and hearts we hold,
In elation's gentle fold.

Laughter's Light

In every smile, a spark ignites,
A beacon through the darkest nights,
With laughter's light, our hearts take flight,
Dispelling shadows, pure delight.

Through fields of green, our spirits soar,
With every joke, we open doors,
A joy that echoes evermore,
In love and laughter, we explore.

Around the fire, stories spun,
With every word, a new day's sun,
With laughter shared by everyone,
The ties that bind cannot be undone.

In moments shared, our souls unite,
In beams of laughter, spirits bright,
Each giggle echoes through the night,
A dance of joy, pure and light.

As moonrise cradles stars above,
We bask in light, a gift of love,
With laughter's light, the heavens move,
In endless dreams, our hearts improve.

Sunshine Within

Inside where shadows fear to tread,
Awakens light from heart's delight,
The quiet warmth in souls is bred,
A beacon in the darkest night.

In every smile, a spark ignites,
Hope risen high, unserved by fate,
Through trials harsh, our spirit fights,
To conquer doubt, and love create.

A gentle whisper, soft and kind,
Dispels the clouds of fear and woe,
Truth's gentle glow in heart we find,
And courage learned in life's tableau.

Beneath the storm, a calm persists,
A steadfast strength, forever true,
From deep within, the soul insists,
That every storm we can subdue.

With every dawn, begins anew,
The day with possibilities,
For in our hearts, the sunshine grew,
And warmth beyond all boundaries.

Fragments of Bliss

In moments caught between the sighs,
A tender laugh, a fleeting glance,
The joy beneath the quiet skies,
In simple things, our hearts entrance.

A leaf that whispers in the breeze,
The shimmer of the morning dew,
Find bliss in these simplicities,
The beauty in the world's milieu.

Through windows wide, life's colors spill,
A palette grand, an endless hue,
Each fragment of a joy instills,
A memory in shades anew.

The song of life, in chords distinct,
Resonates within our chest,
In every beat, our hearts are linked,
The moments cherished, truly blessed.

Collect these fragments, weave a tale,
Of happiness pure, serene,
For through such bliss, we shall prevail,
And find life's peace, unseen.

Serenity In Bloom

In gardens where the silence speaks,
Where petals form the softest kiss,
The quiet hum of days and weeks,
In bloom, serenity exists.

Each flower tells a story old,
In colors bright, in whispers low,
Of mornings kissed by dawn's soft gold,
And twilight's tender, gentle glow.

Beneath the canopy of green,
A world of calm, profound, serene,
Its beauty in each leaf is seen,
A haven from the harsh and mean.

The gentle stream that flows nearby,
In soothing tones, a lullaby,
Its waters clear reflect the sky,
In tranquil waves that never die.

Amidst this quiet, find your peace,
In nature's arms, your soul release,
For in each bloom, our burdens cease,
And all our worries find surcease.

Dancing with Euphoria

In rhythm's embrace, our spirits soar,
To realms where joy and laughter reign,
Each step a poem on the floor,
In euphoria, we break our chains.

A twirl, a leap, heartbeats align,
To melodies both bold and sweet,
In dances woven, love divine,
Through every pulse, our souls compete.

With every beat, the world is new,
A symphony of light and grace,
The stars themselves within our view,
In orbit round this sacred space.

Our worries melt, dissolve in time,
As music's whisper guides our flight,
Euphoria's touch, so pure, sublime,
Transforms the night to endless light.

So let us dance, embrace the fire,
Of joy that sets our hearts afire,
In euphoria we find entire,
A love that lifts us ever higher.

Blooming with Glee

In the garden so wild and free,
Colors dance and leaves swing with spree.
Petals burst with tender plea,
Nature whispers, "Bloom with glee."

Sunlight drips like golden rain,
Washing away every pain.
Birds take flight on skyward lane,
Joy in bloom they do regain.

Morning dew on grass does stay,
A crystal touch to light the day.
Butterflies in skies do sway,
Life anew finds its way.

Trees with shrouds of green embrace,
Branches swaying, heart's own pace.
Flowers trace a loving lace,
Nature's bliss in every place.

Hearts will beat in harmony,
Beneath the skies so wild, so free.
In the blooms we find decree,
Of endless love and boundless glee.

Gratitude in Every Moment

Thankful hearts in morning's light,
Soft whispers break the night.
Gratitude in every sight,
Embrace the day with all your might.

Every breath a gift so rare,
Moments fleeting, handle with care.
Life's rich tapestry we share,
Gratitude is ever fair.

Ripples danced on lake's still face,
Nature's rhythm, a gentle grace.
In every small and quiet space,
Gratitude sets its pace.

Sunset hues in skies ignite,
Painting day to night's delight.
The heart's compass, ever bright,
Gratitude is our guiding light.

Every cause for joy or plea,
Teaches eyes and hearts to see.
In the pulse of life's decree,
Gratitude will set us free.

The Symphony of Delight

Morning breaks with whispers sweet,
Nature's song a rhythmic beat.
Chirping birds and rustling feet,
Compose the day's acoustic treat.

Leaves that rustle, streams that flow,
A symphony both high and low.
Winds that whisper, seeds that sow,
Melodies that always grow.

Footsteps on a pebbled lane,
Joining in the sweet refrain.
Heartbeats echo, peace attain,
Music softens every pain.

Voices merge in sweet delight,
Casting shadows into light.
Every note and chord in sight,
Harmonize with day and night.

In this world where sounds unite,
Melodies take joyous flight.
Nature's song both strong and slight,
Is the symphony of delight.

Inner Sunshine

Golden rays of morning light,
Chase away the dark of night.
Heart and soul begin their flight,
Bathed in ever-warming light.

Thoughts as bright as summer's gleam,
Flow like waters of a dream.
In the mind's own radiant stream,
Sunshine fuels each glowing theme.

Hope within like fire's glow,
Brightens paths where shadows grow.
Inner joy will always show,
Lighting hearts through high and low.

Strength resides within the core,
Opens up each hidden door.
Inner sunshine, evermore,
Guides through life's uncharted shore.

Every soul a star does find,
In the darkness, purely shined.
Inner light and peace combined,
Forms the sunshine in the mind.

The Dance of Joy

In fields of green, under skies so blue,
Hearts once heavy now feel light like dew.
Feet touch the ground with a gentle sway,
Embracing the love of a brand-new day.

Laughter echoes through the open air,
Whirling and twirling without a care.
Fingers intertwine like roots of trees,
In the dance of joy, we find our ease.

Sunlight dapples on every face,
In this sacred, boundless space.
Eyes meet eyes, with a knowing glance,
Celebrating life in a blissful trance.

Songs of nature fill the vibrant scene,
A symphony that's rich, yet serene.
Time stands still in this joyous flight,
Elevated, we take in the light.

In the dance of joy, we all belong,
Each heart beating like a timeless song.
Unified by rhythm, spirit, and cheer,
This dance of joy holds all that's dear.

In the Light of Happiness

In the light of happiness we roam,
Finding solace in each other's home.
Where smiles reflect the morning sun,
Shared joy in which we are all one.

Golden rays upon our path do shine,
Guiding us to moments so divine.
Holding hands, we journey far and wide,
In the light of happiness, we confide.

Whispers of the past melt away,
As we embrace the gift of today.
Hearts aligned, like stars in the night,
In this radiance, everything feels right.

Love blooms through words and deeds,
Nourishing our souls like planted seeds.
We gather strength in this glowing sphere,
A beacon of love, to all we endear.

In the light of happiness we soar,
Bound by joy, forevermore.
There is no end to this gentle flight,
In love's pure and glowing light.

Glistening Moments

Glistening moments captured in time,
Jewels in the memory's endless climb.
Reflections dance like prisms of light,
Casting rainbows in the darkest night.

Each second carries a spark so rare,
A fleeting treasure, beyond compare.
In the heart, these glistening gems reside,
Carved in the soul, there they abide.

Whispers of joy in a gentle breeze,
Moments that bring the heart to ease.
Emotions entwined like morning mist,
In these glistening moments, life persists.

Laughter sparkles like morning dew,
Holding promises pure and true.
Eyes meet eyes, an unspoken rite,
Turning ordinary into delight.

In glistening moments, worlds unfold,
Stories of love and courage told.
A tapestry woven in light's embrace,
Leaving marks only time can trace.

Sparkles of Delight

In the silence of night, stars ignite,
Filling the sky with sparkles of delight.
A dance of light in the velvet dome,
Guiding lost souls back to their home.

Each sparkle a wish, an aspiration,
Mirroring life's endless fascination.
Hopes that glimmer in the silent dark,
Like tiny flames igniting a spark.

Eyes look up with wonder and awe,
In the beauty our spirits draw.
Mysteries unfold in the star's soft glow,
In sparkles of delight, we come to know.

Dreams take flight in this celestial space,
Chasing shadows, setting the pace.
In this realm, our hearts find might,
Fueled by the sparkles of delight.

Together we journey in starlit night,
Bound by dreams so pure and bright.
In the cosmic dance, our fears take flight,
Embracing the magic of sparkles' light.

The Path to Joy

Upon the hills where sunlight beams,
We walk through meadows wide
And chase the echoes of our dreams,
With hope our faithful guide.

Through whispering woods and rivers clear,
The journey leads us far
With laughter's song upon our ear,
As bright as any star.

In every step, the world reveals
A hidden, wondrous view,
For joy resides in simple thrills,
In colors fresh and new.

With each new dawn, horizons shine,
A canvas yet to fill,
And on this journey, hearts entwine,
With strength of purest will.

So let us tread this path with glee,
Despite the trials we face,
For joy, like light, will set us free,
In its warm embrace.

Wonders of a Happy Life

In morning's glow and twilight's hush,
Life's moments softly blend.
With every laugh, with every blush,
Our hearts seem to ascend.

The wonders of a happy soul,
Are not in riches found,
But in the bonds that make us whole,
In love that knows no bound.

We find the magic in each day,
In simple acts of care,
In every word we kindly say,
In dreams we choose to share.

The joys of life are painted bright,
In colors rich and bold,
In friendships warm, and pure delight,
In stories gently told.

Thus let us cherish every beat,
Of hearts that dance as one,
For in this life, so wondrous sweet,
True happiness is spun.

Euphoria's Embrace

In euphoria's warm embrace,
Our spirits rise and soar
To realms of light, a boundless space,
Where dreams are so much more.

The world, a canvas vast and wide,
Awaits our brush and hue,
With joy and passion as our guide,
We paint with colors true.

In every note of nature's song,
We find a melody,
A rhythm pure, where we belong,
In perfect harmony.

Each moment wrapped in blissful air,
We breathe with hearts aglow,
For in this joy, so pure, so rare,
Our lives in beauty flow.

Let euphoria gently weave,
Its threads through all we own,
And in its loving arms, believe
Our happiness has grown.

A Tapestry of Smiles

A tapestry of smiles we weave,
With colors bold and bright,
Each thread a moment we believe,
In kindness, joy, and light.

Through laughter shared and tears embraced,
Our bonds grow strong and deep,
In every heart where love is traced,
A treasure we shall keep.

With every smile, a story told,
Of triumph, hope, and grace,
In golden threads that we behold,
A warm, familiar face.

In times of light, in times of trial,
We hold to what is true,
A world adorned in every smile,
With beauty ever new.

So let us weave, with hands so sure,
This tapestry of life,
With smiles that in our hearts endure,
Through joy and even strife.

A Heart Unburdened

In shadows deep, a heavy chest,
Where dreams had once found lasting rest,
Awaits a spark, a gentle touch,
To lift the weight that clings too much.

Beneath the stars, a silent plea,
For wings to set the spirit free,
The chains of sorrow slowly break,
A heart unburdened, comes awake.

Rivers flow and winds do sway,
Night turns bright with the break of day,
Hope, a phoenix, rises bold,
In this heart, new stories told.

An echo of the past, now gone,
With light and love, the dusk withdrawn,
In every beat, a song refreshed,
A soul in peace, forever blessed.

One step forward, truth embraced,
With every fear and doubt erased,
A journey starts, destiny charted,
A heart unburdened, fearless-hearted.

The Bright Path

Upon the dawn, the light does gleam,
Awakening a hopeful dream,
A path ahead, so clear and bright,
Guiding steps in soft twilight.

Footprints marked on dewy grass,
Leave behind the darkened past,
Each ray of sun, a whispered cheer,
Beckoning the spirit near.

Mountains high and valleys low,
With courage, onward they will go,
Through trials faced and victories won,
Hearts aligned with the rising sun.

A journey carved in golden light,
Promises of pure delight,
Every twist and turn explored,
New horizons to be adored.

Coming forth from shadows cast,
With wisdom learned from lessons past,
The bright path leads to endless days,
In a future, brightened by its rays.

Moments of Wonder

In fleeting seconds, life's embraced,
With wonder found in every space,
Glimmers in a child's wide eyes,
As dreams ascend to endless skies.

A whispered breeze, a fragrant bloom,
An artist's canvas, hues consume,
Nature's dance in the soft embrace,
Of moments painting time and place.

Starry nights where secrets sleep,
In silence, promises they keep,
With every blink, a story told,
Of ancient truths and mysteries old.

Laughter shared, a symphony,
Of joy and pure serendipity,
Connections formed in brief delight,
With hearts alight in the moon's soft light.

Moments fleeting, yet eternal,
Crafting tales, both sublime and thermal,
In these wonders, life does spin,
A universe of magic within.

Whispers of Elation

In dawn's embrace, a silent cheer,
Whispers of elation near,
A heart that hums in tender sound,
With joy in every breath profound.

The morning dew on blades of green,
Reflects a dance, serene and keen,
Solace found in gentle light,
As daybreak holds the promise tight.

Laughter echoes, bubbling free,
An orchestra of harmony,
Waves of joy in moments small,
The beauty in life's tranquil thrall.

In twilight's glow, the whispers rise,
Elation found in evening skies,
Stars like diamonds, crisp and clear,
Sing to those who choose to hear.

In every pulse, the world does sing,
A melody of life in spring,
With every whisper, hearts elate,
Embracing all that love creates.

Boundless Bliss

In fields where wildflowers sing,
Soft breezes weave their gentle tale.
The world in twilight, whispers bring,
A sense of joy that can't but prevail.

Stars twinkle in a moonlit serenade,
While dreams of old and new entwine.
Hearts soar high, free and unafraid,
In boundless bliss, our spirits shine.

Dawn breaks with a delicate grace,
Chasing shadows from the night.
In every warm, sunlit embrace,
We find our peace, we find our light.

Laughter echoes through the trees,
Clouds part to reveal the sky.
We lose ourselves in moments like these,
Where boundless bliss and love reside.

With every breath, a silent prayer,
To hold this joy and never part.
In boundless bliss, we find our share,
Of heaven nestled in the heart.

Cherishing the Joy

Morning whispers through the mist,
Promises of a day so new.
Every dawn a gentle twist,
Cherishing joy in every hue.

Children's laughter, pure and clear,
Echoes through the open air.
In their eyes, no hint of fear,
Only joy beyond compare.

Nature hums her timeless song,
Waves that kiss the sandy shore.
Moments fleeting, but so strong,
Cherishing joy forevermore.

Amidst the rush, we pause to find,
Simple pleasures, soft and sweet.
Cherishing joy in heart and mind,
In every moment where we meet.

Hand in hand, through seasons' flow,
Together in this sacred dance.
Cherishing joy as we grow,
In every fleeting, precious chance.

Rays of Felicity

Sunlight streams through autumn leaves,
Casting shadows, warm and bright.
Rays of felicity one perceives,
In the heart of morning light.

Laughter fills the golden space,
Echoing through a world reborn.
Rays of joy, an embrace,
Felicity in each new dawn.

In simple acts of kindness shared,
A smile, a touch, a helping hand.
Rays of felicity declared,
Across this vast and tender land.

The day unfolds in radiant beams,
Guiding us through paths unknown.
Rays of hope in fragile dreams,
Felicity in seeds we've sown.

As twilight wraps the earth in grace,
Stars emerge to light the sky.
Rays of felicity we embrace,
In endless joy that lifts us high.

Unveiling the Gladness

Morning dew on petals rests,
A new day in soft embrace.
Unveiling gladness in each jest,
Nature's joy, a quiet grace.

Songs of birds at break of day,
Harmonies that warm the soul.
Unveiling gladness in their play,
Moments that make us whole.

Through each challenge, strength we find,
In the touch of hope so true.
Unveiling gladness in the mind,
And skies no longer blue.

Warmth of friendship, hand in hand,
Unyielding through life's stormy sea.
Unveiling gladness in this band,
Of hearts forever free.

Evenings bring a gentle hush,
Stars appear, a glittered trace.
Unveiling gladness in the blush,
Of night's tender, calm embrace.

The Happiness You Seek

In the quiet of the morning light,
Where dreams and waking gently meet,
There lies the happiness you seek,
In moments soft and pure delight.

Trace the path where shadows fade,
And sunlight dances on the stream,
Here, the universe conspires,
To bless you with the love you crave.

Feel the whispers in the breeze,
As laughter echoes through the air,
These are the treasures of your heart,
Every smile, a precious piece.

In the kindness of a stranger's gaze,
And in the warmth of a friend's embrace,
Find the joy that never wanes,
In the simple, lovely ways.

The happiness you seek is near,
In the grace of every day,
Lift your eyes and you will see,
It has always been here to stay.

Echoes of Delight

In the forest deep and green,
Where sunlight filters through the leaves,
Echoes of delight are found,
In whispers soft and moments keen.

A bird's song flits through the air,
Notes of joy that freely soar,
In nature's symphony of love,
Lies the magic, pure and fair.

The river's laughter as it flows,
Among the rocks in playful dance,
A melody of time and grace,
Holding secrets no one knows.

Beneath the stars' eternal glow,
The night unveils its gentle charms,
In dreams and wishes quietly sown,
In the comfort of the dark.

With each step in life's embrace,
Feel the echoes soft and bright,
In every heart that dares to love,
Lie the seeds of pure delight.

Journey to Joy

On the path where dreams align,
With hopes as bright as morning's rays,
Begin the journey to your joy,
With open heart and ready mind.

Each step you take in trust and love,
A tapestry of moments sews,
Free from shadows of the past,
Find the light that lies above.

In the laughter shared with friends,
And the kindness given free,
Seek the beauty of the world,
Through the love that never ends.

Embrace the rhythm of your soul,
Let it guide each day anew,
Through valleys deep and mountains high,
Feel the joy that makes you whole.

The journey to joy's path unfolds,
In every breath, in every choice,
In the harmony of life,
Find the song your heart beholds.

Radiance Unbound

In dawn's first gentle touch of light,
A promise of the day unfolds,
Radiance unbound and pure,
A universe in hues of bright.

The sky ablaze with morning's fire,
A canvas painted every hue,
Whispers of the night's embrace,
Melt away in dawn's desire.

In each bloom that welcomes sun,
Petals soft and colors bold,
Find the heart's unspoken dreams,
In every blossom, joy is spun.

A smile shared, a moment stilled,
In the glow of love's own light,
Radiance unbound and true,
Holds the world in beauty's thrill.

Through the daylight's golden arc,
And the twilight's whispered song,
Feel the radiance of the heart,
As it carries life along.

Soaring Spirits

Above the clouds, we glide in flight,
With wings outstretched, we seize the light.
The wind's embrace, a tender kiss,
In endless skies, we find pure bliss.

Through sapphire seas, on currents strong,
We chase the sun where dreams belong.
Hearts alight with joy untold,
In boundless realms of blue and gold.

Our spirits free, untamed, unbound,
In azure heights, our truths are found.
The heavens whisper secrets dear,
In soaring heights, the world is clear.

Together, we defy the ground,
In unity, our souls are crowned.
The earth below, a distant dream,
In endless flight, we reign supreme.

With wings of hope and hearts of fire,
We soar above, we rise, aspire.
In boundless skies, our spirits sing,
For in this flight, we are the king.

The Garden of Mirth

In gardens where the blossoms beam,
We find our joy, a pure daydream.
Each petal spreads a tale of cheer,
A fragrant song, we hold so dear.

Laughter echoes through the glade,
In sunlight's kiss and dappled shade.
The breeze, a whisper soft and kind,
In every leaf, delight we find.

Beneath the trees, where shadows play,
Our hearts engage in merry fray.
With every step, the earth does sing,
In harmony with birds on wing.

Rivulets of happiness run free,
Through verdant grass, past every tree.
In this garden, life abounds,
With joy and love, our souls are crowned.

Together here, in nature's arms,
We revel in its countless charms.
The garden blooms with endless birth,
A sacred space of boundless mirth.

In peace we dwell, in joy we thrive,
In this garden, we're alive.
With nature's touch, in pure delight,
We bask in day, embrace the night.

A Radiant Collection

A gallery of stars above,
In twilight skies, they speak of love.
Each shimmer holds a wish profound,
In silent whispers, dreams are found.

The moonlight paints a portrait bright,
Of silvery beams and gentle light.
In night's embrace, we find our peace,
In celestial dance, our hearts release.

Comets blaze with fervent thrill,
Across the heavens, swift and still.
They trail their light in fleeting grace,
A radiant streak in boundless space.

The constellations weave their tales,
Of heroes bold and whispered trails.
In every star, a story shines,
A tapestry of ancient lines.

Together, we gaze up in awe,
At wonders near and sights afar.
In this vast collection, bright and true,
A radiant world, we wander through.

With every glance, a new delight,
In starlit whispers through the night.
A radiant collection, pure,
In every star, our dreams endure.

The Blissful Cascade

Through forest groves and valleys wide,
A river flows, where dreams abide.
Its gentle sound, a lullaby,
In nature's arms, it glides on by.

The waters dance in playful glee,
A mirrored sky, so wild and free.
Each ripple sings a song of peace,
In every wave, our worries cease.

At waterfalls, where currents leap,
The world unfolds in motions deep.
Cascading joy in crystal streams,
A symphony of liquid dreams.

In sunlit pools, we find reprieve,
The waters' touch, our spirits weave.
With every splash, a pure embrace,
In nature's flow, we find our place.

The river winds through night and day,
A silver path, a flowing ray.
In Blissful Cascade, we're renewed,
In every drop, with life imbued.

Together, by its banks we stand,
Our hearts in tune with nature's hand.
The river's song, our endless guide,
In Blissful Cascade, we abide.

Unchained Joy

Freedom dances in the breeze
Unseen but deeply felt
Laughter echoes through the trees
Where once the shadows dwelt

New horizons spread their wings
Colors rich and bright
The heart, it soars, it truly sings
Into the endless light

Smiles bloom like summer's flowers
Beauty unconfined
Moments stretch like golden hours
In the tapestry of mind

Joy unchained from sorrow's grasp
Rides on winds anew
In the purest peace, we clasp
A world decked in true view

Dreams are painted, vivid, bold
On the canvas high
Unchained joy, a story told
Beneath the boundless sky

The Harmony Within

In silence, whispers find their voice
A symphony unseen
Heartbeats sync, the spirits rejoice
In tranquil, serene

The soul's melody softly plays
In the quiet room
Harmonic threads of yesterdays
In every tender bloom

Peaceful chords align the mind
Like rivers gently flow
Within the calm, the truth we find
Where inner gardens grow

Each breath a note, each sigh a song
In harmony, we're whole
Infinite calm where we belong
In the depths of the soul

The inner music of the heart
Resonates pure and true
When all in life seems to depart
Within, we start anew

Blooming Joy

Petals open to the sun
Colors bright and fair
Every smile, a bloom begun
In the fragrant air

Moments painted with delight
Like blossoms in the field
Joy emerging, pure and bright
In each embrace revealed

Laughter springs from every seed
Happiness in bloom
In the garden, hearts are freed
Dispelling all the gloom

Nature's palette, strokes of grace
In every flower's glow
In the meadow, life's embrace
Where endless wonders show

Blooming joy, a season's gift
In every heart it stays
A gentle, warm and tender lift
To brighten all our days

The Beat of Bliss

Rhythms pulse beneath the skin
A dancer to life's song
Every heartbeat lets us in
To where true joys belong

The drum of bliss, so deep and clear
Echoes through the veins
Cascades of laughter we hold dear
Like warm, refreshing rains

Steps of pleasure, dance of cheer
On life's vast, open floor
With each beat, the path grows near
To hearts we so adore

Voices raised in jubilant praise
In harmony we sing
The beat of bliss in clouds of rays
To every moment cling

With the pulse of cherished dreams
We live in light and grace
In the beat of bliss, it seems
We find our sacred place

The Warm Embrace

In fields where whispers grow,
Soft winds among the trees,
A touch as light as snow,
Awake the gentle breeze.

In twilight's soft embrace,
The stars begin to peek,
A calm within this place,
Where hearts and spirits speak.

The night, it calls so sweet,
A lullaby's refrain,
With every heart's soft beat,
Two souls, they feel no pain.

The moonlight gently spills,
On lovers' intertwined,
The warmth, it softly fills,
Two spirits now aligned.

In memories so dear,
Where timeless love resides,
They hold each other near,
No distance in divides.

Tranquil Hearts

Beside the quiet stream,
Where waters gently flow,
We lay in peaceful dream,
As time begins to slow.

The whispers of the breeze,
Through leaves they softly sing,
A hymn of ancient trees,
Where nature's heart will ring.

The sunlight filters down,
In beams through canopies,
As nature wears its crown,
In hues of golden seas.

With hearts that beat in tune,
To earth's eternal song,
We find beneath the moon,
Where tranquil hearts belong.

In stillness we will find,
The beauty life imparts,
A bond that's purely kind,
A love in tranquil hearts.

The Glow of Hope

In shadows deep and long,
Where darkness tries to creep,
A light, both bright and strong,
Ensures we do not weep.

It flickers in the night,
A beacon in despair,
With glow, so soft and bright,
To show us love's still there.

The weary find their rest,
In glimmers of its flame,
It warms the hollow breast,
And quells the fear and shame.

A hope that never dies,
Though storms may rage and roar,
It lights the cloudy skies,
And guides us evermore.

In every soul it lives,
This glow that's ever bright,
A gift that freely gives,
To pierce the darkest night.

Delight in Every Step

With every step we take,
A world unfolds anew,
In paths that gently wake,
The wonders in our view.

The morning's fresh sunrise,
A canvas painted gold,
Where endless beauty lies,
Our hearts, it does enfold.

In laughter's joyous sound,
And whispers of the earth,
Delight in steps profound,
We find our truest worth.

The petals soft and sweet,
The breeze that passes by,
In moments where we meet,
Delight that fills the sky.

With every step, we find,
A joy that's boundless, free,
Within our heart and mind,
A pure, unspoken glee.

Milton Keynes UK
Ingram Content Group UK Ltd.
UKHW050130270624
444593UK00005BA/61

9 789916 756706